We are in the midst of a very serious period of cul
instability. And make no mistake about it: the Chu
solving these problems. This guided study offers a
read and put into practice the ideas it presents, you cannot help but be an informed part of the solution, to the honor of Jesus Christ and the good of our brothers and sisters. I am so grateful that this is now available.

J. P. MORELAND, PHD
Distinguished Professor of Philosophy
Talbot School of Theology, Biola University

I genuinely can't express how grateful and relieved I am that the Center for Biblical Unity has produced this small-group curriculum. There are a lot of churches that want to facilitate groups on racial unity, but the most popular books and curricula are either wholly unbiblical or are a confusing mix of biblical and unbiblical concepts. This is the ONE curriculum I've seen that is spot on—unashamedly leaving behind secular ideas about race and speaking to the truth of God's Word. What a breath of fresh air!

NATASHA CRAIN
Speaker, blogger, author, and host of *The Natasha Crain Podcast*

Monique Duson has given the church a unique and timely resource. While the culture searches for a way to address racism and inequality, Christ-followers are struggling to evaluate Critical Race Theory in light of the teaching of Jesus. *Reconciled: A Biblical Approach to Racial Unity* will help Christians form a foundation for the unity we have in Christ as we come to understand the healing power of the Gospel.

J. WARNER WALLACE
Dateline-featured cold-case detective,
Senior Fellow at the Colson Center for Christian Worldview,
Adjunct Professor of Apologetics at Talbot School of Theology (Biola University),
and author of *Cold-Case Christianity* and *Person of Interest*

This is the curriculum I've been waiting for! Discussions surrounding racism and injustice in the body of Christ have not always been fruitful or productive. With such a sensitive topic that affects us all in different ways, we can often end up talking past one another or adopting unbiblical solutions. The curriculum from the Center for Biblical Unity will help facilitate meaningful conversations that will lead Christians of all ethnic backgrounds toward healing, unity, and biblical faithfulness.

ALISA GIRARD CHILDERS
Author, *Another Gospel*

This study by Monique Duson is desperately needed for both the Church and for a world divided by the sin of racism. Monique—a woman once committed to Critical Race Theory and since transformed by the power of the Spirit—offers a thoroughly biblical solution to the problem of racism. I am proud to call Monique sister and to walk alongside every member of our Family in pursuit of the holiness found only in the cross of Christ.

DR. JOE "J. R." MILLER
President and co-founder of the Center for Cultural Apologetics

Finally! Evangelical Christians have desperately needed a scriptural and sensible Bible study on racial unity, and Monique Duson has provided exactly that with *Reconciled: A Biblical Approach to Racial Unity*! Monique graciously guides readers into understanding the real reasons for racial disunity and how the correct understanding and then application of Scripture result in biblical unity. *Reconciled* shows non-Christians their need to be reconciled to God, and Christian readers will find Monique's arguments accessible, enlightening, compelling, and even comforting.

DR. CLAY JONES
Visiting scholar at Talbot School of Theology,
chairman of the board of Ratio Christi, and author of *Why Does God Allow Evil?: Compelling Answers for Life's Toughest Questions*; clayjones.net.

The current challenges facing our society have proven again that there is no moral neutrality in culture. To assume that there is would derail a Christian from his or her call to defend truth necessary to create an "authentic public square." This curriculum provides the groundwork necessary to equip believers not only to confront cultural deviations on the issue of racism but also to actualize true biblical reconciliation within their spheres of influence. I recommend it to anyone who is seeking to have a faithful presence and fulfill their call to build a flourishing society for all on the foundation of the Word of God.

DR. JACOB DANIEL
Founder, Heritage Counsel

Monique has created a study that teaches Christians to prioritize their identity in Christ first, to discuss racial issues with love and compassion, and to treat others as fellow image-bearers of God. Contrary to the culture's lies and damaging attempts at reconciliation through Critical Race Theory, this group study is full of biblical truth and the answer to achieving true unity—the blood of Jesus Christ.

RACHEL SHOCKEY
President, Women In Apologetics

Brilliant! Pastors and Christian leaders, I implore you, take your people through this timely, relevant, thoughtfully organized, interactive, and deeply biblical curriculum immediately. In doing so, you will prepare them to stand for truth against a hostile cultural ideology that is pressing in on every side. Here you will find deep wisdom on pressing issues of our day: race and racism, racial reconciliation, and biblical unity. Monique understands more than most that biblical truth and critical theory are distinct and incompatible worldviews. One bears the good fruit of peace, unity, and reconciliation—the other the bitter fruit of division, grievance, and hostility.

SCOTT DAVID ALLEN
President, Disciple Nations Alliance, and author of *Why Social Justice Is Not Biblical Justice: An Urgent Appeal to Fellow Christians in a Time of Social Crisis*

Critical race theory promises antiracism and unity—this is one of the reasons that it's so enticing to many Christians. However, though it promises antiracism, it delivers racism. Though it promises unity, it delivers division. This is why I'm especially grateful for *Reconciled: A Biblical Approach to Racial Unity* by my dear friends at the Center for Biblical Unity. They do not merely stand against Critical Race Theory—they stand for Christ and his Church. This is why they've created this sincere, sanctifying, and succinct curriculum about unity in Christ. This is a valuable resource for me, and I'm sure it will be the same for you.

SAMUEL SEY
Blogger, SlowToWrite.com

Reconciled is a perfect, practical representation of "setting your minds on things that are above" (Colossians 3). As believers, we have a duty to discern well the lies of the enemy. This curriculum places the scriptures front and center while engaging in hard topics—a freedom afforded to those truly reconciled to the Creator of all things. This study accentuates the present reality of the church while pointing toward its eternal reality—a divine family. Through this curriculum, we're reminded that the divine reality is actualized. Praise God!

BRANDON SMITH
Pastor and Co-host, *Black and Blurred* podcast
and
DAREN SMITH
Worship Leader and Co-host, *Black and Blurred* podcast

As someone who once held a firm belief in Critical Race Theory (CRT) and "wokeness," Monique Duson shares a unique perspective, having firsthand knowledge of why this worldview would be so enticing to so many. Monique's work on this curriculum is significant to the body of Christ. Racial reconciliation has been purchased through Christ, and this material is reflective of that understanding.

VIRGIL WALKER, MBA
Executive Director, G3 Ministries
Co-host, *Just Thinking Podcast*

RECONCILED

A BIBLICAL APPROACH TO RACIAL UNITY

MONIQUE DUSON

Foreword by J. P. Moreland

A CENTER FOR BIBLICAL UNITY CURRICULUM

Reconciled

Published in the United States of America by Credo House Publishers,
a division of Credo Communications LLC, Grand Rapids, Michigan
credohousepublishers.com

ISBN: 978-1-62586-226-6

Interior by Sharon VanLoozenoord
Editing by Donna Huisjen

Printed in the United States of America
First edition

Center for Biblical Unity
P.O. Box 811
Upland, CA 91785

CenterForBiblicalUnity.com

CONTENTS

FOREWORD

It's been my honor to meet and hear from Monique Duson, the founder and president of Center for Biblical Unity. Monique is uniquely qualified to write the study you hold in your hands. Raised and educated in an environment of Critical Race Theory, along with associated ideologies, Monique knows firsthand how false and ineffective this soul-deadening approach really is. She found herself getting more and more angry as she grew distant from God and His Word. Fortunately, she began studying and immersing herself in a biblically grounded worldview with a focus on how this informs the racial situation that plagues us today. As a result, she has become a knowledgeable leader in the movement to enlist the Church and fellow believers in the cause of biblical justice, diversity, and racial reconciliation.

What is so refreshing, so hopeful, and so desperately needed is an approach to these and related topics that embodies a clear dedication to discipleship unto the Lord Jesus, to living in a manner worthy of His Kingdom, and to the authority of the very Word of God. In the pages to follow, we are time and time again led back to a careful examination of Scripture regarding one difficult topic after another. In order to make scriptural teaching appear as relevant and profound as it actually is, Monique regularly contrasts the contemporary cultural approach, one that is Neo-Marxist at its core, with a biblical approach. The result not only exposes the reader to the false, harmful, and Christ-dishonoring cultural approach; it also shines a light on the stunning insight the Bible offers into the real underlying causes of our current crisis.

This study is exactly the tool that the Church needs. It is brief and concise, while being meaty and deep. It refocuses the reader's attention on a distinctively Christian way to approach the topics within its purview. And it offers additional resources for additional reflection. This study is ideal for individual and/

or group interaction, and my prayer is that, after you read it, you will spread the word to others and encourage groups to form around it.

We are in the midst of a very serious period of cultural chaos, division, and instability. And make no mistake about it: the Church is our best hope for solving these problems. This guided study offers a hopeful way out. If you read and put into practice the ideas it presents, you cannot help but be an informed part of the solution, to the honor of Jesus Christ and the good of our brothers and sisters. I am so grateful that this is now available.

J. P. MORELAND, PHD
Distinguished Professor of Philosophy
Talbot School of Theology
Biola University

INTRODUCTION

Let's be honest. America has an ugly history with racism, prejudice, and injustice. Slavery. Native American genocide. Segregation. Redlining. Japanese, German, and Italian internment camps. And there's more. Some say that America has been racist since its beginning—that *racism* is our country's "original sin."

But an ugly history marked by ethnic mistreatment doesn't make our country unique. A few *recent* historical examples from around the world include the clashes between the Tutsis and Hutus in the Rwandan genocide, the Yugoslav Wars, the bloody conflict between the Tamils and Sinhalese of Sri Lanka, and Nazism. Issues with racism have existed since the earliest days of human history. They have affected the treatment of most, if not all, people groups. In many countries, racism goes largely unchecked and results in the deaths of thousands of innocent people, all of them made in God's image, every year.

The United States has passed many laws to ensure fair and equal treatment and help us overcome our racist past. Yet today's cultural narrative suggests that America is *more* racist, and more racially divided, than at any other moment in history.

From both inside and outside the Church, we can hear cries for racial justice. Inside the Church, many preachers are issuing calls for "racial reconciliation" and demanding that white people lament and repent of their "whiteness" and support the Marxist-led organization Black Lives Matter. Outside the Church, cancel culture waits to take down anyone who disagrees.

Some proponents of Critical Race Theory and social justice advocate that racism is not actually the most foundational problem. Rather, they claim, race issues stem from a deeper, more pervasive problem that has burrowed itself into the fabric of American life: whiteness. *Whiteness* refers to the invisible values and privileges granted to white people based solely on their skin color. According to this theory, whiteness is what allows racism and the oppression of people of color to continue unchecked in nearly every facet of American life, including banking, education, law, and medicine. This, so the argument goes, is why social media is filled with cries that America continues to be a racist country.

To combat the oppression created by whiteness, leaders—from Fortune 500 companies to small nonprofit organizations—are having conversations about race and are instituting diversity, equity, and inclusion trainings. Many evangelical churches, ministries, and universities are doing the same.

This study guide takes a different approach. Our goal is to provide a solid biblical foundation for racial unity that helps Christians focus less on what divides us and more on what unites us.

WHY CAN'T WE JUST GET ALONG?

Have you ever watched two people who speak different languages try to communicate? Speaking slowly, they may raise their voices in the effort to be understood, hoping that greater volume will somehow bring greater clarity. Hand gestures and eye-rolling, visible signs of frustration, may also signify their inability to connect.

Miscommunication has caused several tense conversations between my ministry partner, Krista, and me. When we first started discussing race, justice, and unity, I assumed she knew the *right* definitions to the words I used. Doesn't *everyone* know that racism equals prejudice plus power?

But Krista didn't. Much of the time, I'd raise my voice, hoping to help her "get it." She called it "yelling."

Among the greatest problems facing conversations about racial reconciliation is a lack of clear definitions. Terms and phrases that used to mean one thing have been redefined. In the past, words like "racism" connoted someone's personal actions or heart posture against another individual. Today this term refers to group power and systematic discrimination that have become ordinary and embedded throughout society and culture. Without the awareness of changed definitions, you may find yourself using terms in a manner inconsistent with their revised meaning, or, worse yet, you may end up speaking right past your friends and loved ones in conversation.

To make sure this group uses the same definitions, we've included a short glossary at the back of this study guide.

BASIC ASSUMPTIONS FOR THIS STUDY

Before diving into our study, we should probably clarify three key assumptions that will undergird its framework. The ideas presented in each lesson are shared with these beliefs in mind.

The Bible Is Our Authority

> By his divine power, God has given us *everything we need for living a godly life.* We have received all of this by coming to know him, the one who called us to himself by means of his marvelous glory and excellence. (2 Peter 1:3 NLT, emphasis mine)

Scripture is the foremost authority for everything needed for life and godliness. As Christians, we not only have the ability to read and understand the Bible, but we also have the tools necessary to see problems in culture, speak boldly about solutions, and use our voices to speak prophetically about the future. We are to be a city on a hill, participating with God in leading people out of darkness and into His marvelous light. We must look to Scripture to shape our thoughts, feelings, and opinions about how to live a holy life. That will maximize our impact on our culture.

We Are Family

> In love he predestined us for *adoption to sonship* through Jesus Christ, in accordance with his pleasure and will. (Ephesians 1:4b–5, emphasis mine)

Our primary identity is found in Christ, not in our ethnic or racial heritage. When you're a follower of Christ, you've been adopted as a son or daughter into the household of God. Scripture declares that believers are united through the blood of Jesus, accomplished through His work on the cross of Calvary. That makes every believer your brother or sister.

Understanding the reality of our identity is foundational to understanding our relationship to other believers. We are brothers and sisters *first*. Our relationship statuses are not those of oppressed and oppressor. Nor should we base our relationships on any human efforts or work that we can do. Only the perfect work of Jesus could take sinful humans, ethnic enemies, and make them family. We are family—not because of our works, our will, or our ethnicity. We are family because it's God's good pleasure to adopt us as His children.

One Race

> *From one man he made all the nations,* that they should inhabit the whole earth. (Acts 17:26, emphasis mine)

As we attempt to live out the spiritual reality of our relationships as siblings, it's also important to understand our physical reality. Adam and Eve, humanity's first parents, were directly created by God. Since all humans descended from them, there is only one race—the human race. Still, there are several ethnicities.

The term "race" is an unbiblical social construct that came into use between the sixteenth and seventeenth centuries. Prior to that, people were grouped according to familial clan or language. However, with the spread of colonialism, people began being grouped by physical characteristics. Such categories provided a method for dividing humanity and allowing ruling or conquering people groups to subdue and abuse others. That's how race became a social construct. And it's how race became a false foundation for group pride—and for hatred of other groups. When we move away from God toward such attitudes, we tend to seek power and control over one another.

Where We Are Going

As we move through each lesson, we'll look at key passages of Scripture that relate to conversations about race and ethnicity. We'll also take time to learn from each other's stories about our struggles with race-based bias. The hope is that unity will be built into your group and that, as understanding grows, so will friendship.

Each lesson includes a discussion, along with a homework assignment designed to encourage reflection on the discussion's topic. This framework will help participants consider practical ways to apply each lesson to real life.

Participation equals value. Your full participation, within both the study and your small group, will reap the most benefits. I encourage you to dig into Scripture as you go through *Reconciled.* Allow the Bible to be your guide. Get honest with the Holy Spirit and with your group. My prayer is that, while you may come into this as strangers, you'll leave as family.

May the Holy Spirit multiply our love for one another as brothers and sisters in Christ.

Blessings,

Monique Duson

Founder and President, Center for Biblical Unity

FAMILY RULES

Topics like race, justice, and unity are important to discuss, and we are aware that they can be sensitive subjects. As we walk together on this journey, a shared understanding of how we will participate with one another will help provide a space of safety and draw us closer together in our communication.

As we begin, your group may not yet have the relational trust, mutual respect, and security necessary for vulnerable discussions with each other. That's normal. Hopefully, however, after a meeting or two, this dynamic will start to flourish.

If you're a Person of Color, you might feel concerned that other participants—or this study—will try to convince you that racism is a thing of the past. That isn't the case. To be clear, we believe that racism is real and can affect members of every ethnicity in different ways.

If you are a white participant, you might feel concerned that you'll be told you're a racist simply because you are white. We do not believe anyone should be shamed because of their skin's melanin content.

If you are of mixed ethnicity, you may be feeling as though you need to choose a side, or wondering where you fit in the conversation. There is no need to choose. You belong right here, with this group, in this conversation. These lessons aren't geared toward any specific ethnic identity; they are instead constructed from the reality of our identity in Christ.

As trust is being built, be intentional about providing a space for everyone to be heard. Don't place parameters on the group, such as allowing only people of color to recount their racial trauma. Allow the white group members, as well as the people of color, to share their difficult experiences. Encourage mutual respect and empathy for every participant's pain.

We are on this journey together. This may be your very first conversation about race, justice, and unity, or this may be a conversation you regularly have. Whatever your position, we are all entering this conversation with our own unique experiences from unique families, cultures, and histories. Be kind. Be patient.

We won't all have the same knowledge base, and we will all need grace. Regardless of where you find yourself, we are family. These ground rules will help us keep in step with those who are traveling with us.

Every group member should agree to these ground rules before starting:

1. Be respectful.

Being respectful looks like:

- waiting your turn to speak
- being willing to hear people out
- not cursing or yelling at others
- being on time
- giving people the benefit of the doubt
- bearing with one another in patience

2. Suspend judgment.

Judgment looks like:

- labeling people (e.g., fragile, racist, race baiter, naive)
- categorizing people according to their ethnicity
- assuming motivation ("She's speaking from her privilege.")
- dismissing the experiences of others ("That isn't real racism." "You're too sensitive.")

3. Be curious.

Curiosity looks like:

- asking for clarification
- noticing your own biases, judgments, and assumptions
- taking time to do your own research, then bringing your questions to the group

4. Actively participate.

Active participation looks like:

- being honest
- sharing your experience
- listening to the experiences of others
- risking a hard conversation
- staying in the room, even when it's hard

5. Complete the homework.

Completing the homework looks like:

- praying about and answering all homework questions before your next session
- writing out any questions you have about the homework
- leaving behind any judgments you have from the previous week

If you're unable to complete the homework (We get it: life happens!), plan to limit your participation the following week to listening during the homework discussion time.

As a group, feel free to come up with one or two additional ground rules that may help your group thrive in participation and communication.

Discuss any questions about these ground rules. Each member should commit to practicing these boundaries before your group moves forward.

LESSON 1

WHAT IS THE "MINISTRY OF RECONCILIATION"?

WARM UP

Take 10 minutes to read through the ground rules as a group. Address any questions or concerns that may come up.

Many individuals and organizations desiring to combat racial injustice have sought to do so through the method of "racial reconciliation." Some evangelical pastors challenge their congregants to participate in this work. Rarely, though, does anyone stop to ask strategic questions.

In many churches, racial reconciliation generally begins with a convicting message from the lead pastor that recounts the injustices, both past and present, faced by people of color. Often this sermon is accompanied by an admonition or exhortation telling white people how they've been complicit in racism and need to "do better." Then the pastor issues a call to end racism by laying aside white privilege, working against injustice, and becoming antiracist. Often, these calls to action fail to include specifics. But when they are described, they usually mirror secular social-justice ideals.

In this lesson, we'll consider the question "Does the *Church* need to participate in racial reconciliation?"

OPENING DISCUSSION (10 MINUTES)

The core argument for racial reconciliation is usually built on one verse: 2 Corinthians 5:18. We'll look at this verse in just a minute. But first, let's discuss the following questions.

1. What are your biggest concerns about participating in this group? What are you feeling nervous about? Focus on listening to one another's concerns. If we want to fulfill the law of Christ by loving our neighbor as ourselves (Matthew 22:36-40), then we must bear one another's burdens (Galatians 6:2).

____

____

____

____

____

____

Remember, listening and focusing on one another's concerns help us fulfill the law of Christ—loving our neighbor as ourselves.

2. What are you hearing from other members of your group? Are they experiencing any of your fears and emotions? Where do you see some overlap?

____

____

____

Many Christian leaders and ministries are deeply committed to the work of racial reconciliation. This process often requires a series of steps, but these steps vary from model to model. Following is a sampling of the approaches floating around evangelical churches.

MODEL 1:

- **LISTEN** to the experiences of people of color.
- **LAMENT** issues of racism and injustice with people of color.
- **LEGISLATE** the equitable treatment of all people of color.
- **REPENT** from complicity in racist systems and structures.

MODEL 2:

- **COMMITMENT:** Whites must cast off privilege, prestige, comfort, and preference, and they must commit to acting on behalf of the marginalized.
- **AWARENESS:** We must stay "woke" to racial injustice and aware of America's racist history.
- **RELATIONSHIPS:** It is not enough to be aware. To be serious about reconciliation, you must be in relationship with those outside your ethnicity.

MODEL 3:

- **RACIAL RECONCILIATION THROUGH REPARATIONS.** Christian leaders who advocate for racial reconciliation believe that reconciliation can be achieved only as the history of unjust treatment by white Americans against people of color is acknowledged and reparations are paid.

MODEL 4:

- **RACIAL RECONCILIATION THROUGH ANTIRACISM.** This approach focuses on conscious efforts and actions taken to create laws and policies that result in equitable opportunities and outcomes for all people, both individually and systemically.

Do the Work!

IF YOU'VE BEEN around conversations about racial reconciliation for at least ten minutes, you've probably heard the phrase *Do the work*. For most racial-reconciliation proponents, "the work" is that of antiracism: "Educate yourself." "If you're white, speak out." "If you're white, don't speak." (Confused? I am.) "Abolish the patriarchy." "Confront injustice and oppression." "Get woke/stay woke." The "works" list can become long and overwhelming.

We believe that the underlying goal of many Christian racial-reconciliation advocates is to promote the value, dignity, and worth of all individuals. They want to create a level playing field where one ethnicity is not considered higher or treated as more valuable than another. That is a worthy goal.

However, this goal is based on the framework of *naturalism*. This vision of racial reconciliation addresses what we see and understand from a merely natural perspective. It argues that by using human interventions to improve the natural surroundings of others, we'll improve equality. Again, a worthy goal, but not the supreme idea.

Such an approach confronts only the evil we see. But the Christian worldview instructs us that, as long as there are humans, there will always be evil, known and unknown, seen and unseen. Scripture teaches that the intentions of the human heart are always bent toward pride, selfishness, and wickedness. That's why we need a Savior. Until Jesus returns, Christ's followers will always be engaged in the work of combating evil.

This is why the hope of racial unity must begin with repentance, humility, and love: first to Christ, then to others.

Christianity offers a more complete hope for racial unity. The biblical worldview goes beyond the scope of the natural to the supernatural. Christianity understands that the very heart of man is dark and that the Word of God speaks into that place, offering light. A relationship with Jesus is the only secure option for transforming the hearts of individuals. Changed hearts are the only hope for a changed system.

Yes, we must do the work. But the cyclical tool of secular racial reconciliation cannot produce long-lasting, truly transformational fruit. The work we must press toward is all about humility, compassion, forgiveness, grace, and love. *This* is the work of Christ's followers.

3. Select someone to read 2 Corinthians 5:18 aloud. For now, read only verse 18. (We'll look at the surrounding verses later in this lesson.) Has anyone in your group heard this verse used by a pastor to promote racial reconciliation? What steps were used to facilitate the solution?

____

____

____

The specifics of what's entailed in the work of racial reconciliation are often left undefined. A concrete, step-by-step plan for achieving racial harmony is rarely included. Nor are timelines or specific criteria provided for measuring when racial reconciliation has been achieved. Even though many pastors are exhorting their congregations to do the work of racial reconciliation, they are taking their people on a journey in which their striving will likely have no end.

Is there a simpler, more hopeful way to reach racial unity? We say yes!

BIBLE STUDY (35 MINUTES)

Let's take a closer look at the context of 2 Corinthians 5:18 and see what kind of "reconciliation" the Bible describes here.

1. Select someone to read 2 Corinthians 5:10–21 aloud. According to this passage, and verse 18 in particular, who are the two parties in need of reconciliation? Who needs to be reconciled to whom?

____

____

____

2. What exactly is the "ministry of reconciliation" mentioned in verse 18?

____

____

____

3. What is the purpose of this reconciliation? Whom are we trying to persuade? What are we trying to persuade them to do? (Hint: Reread verses 11 and 20.)

____

____

____

4. Looking at verse 19, what message of reconciliation are these ambassadors supposed to bring?

____

____

____

5. Based on your study, write a one-sentence summary of this passage's big idea. What is the thesis for this set of verses?

____

____

____

When looking at verse 18 in its broader context, we see that the ministry of reconciliation given to Christians is about encouraging sinful humans to become reconciled to a holy God. We do this because we respect the Lord and want to persuade others to do the same.

We can also see that 2 Corinthians 5:18 has *nothing* to do with what people today call racial reconciliation. It simply doesn't work to use this verse as the biblical warrant for racial reconciliation as a Christian mandate.

TEACHING (15 MINUTES)

The teaching portion of this lesson builds on our Bible study. Here are a few key points to listen for as you watch the video:

- Racial reconciliation is the wrong primary goal for a Christian.
- Our first obligation is to be reconciled to God.
- We can't begin to talk about unity in the Body of Christ if we don't first understand the condition of our hearts and our need for a holy God.
- Jesus's work on the cross overcame sin, death, and the devil.

 **PLAY** the 15-minute video message "The Myth of Racial Reconciliation" with Monique Duson.

REFLECTION (15 MINUTES)

After watching the video, take a few minutes to process the teaching and hear from each other.

1. What did you find helpful about the teaching?

---

2. Share one idea you heard that was new for you. What other questions does that new idea raise?

---

3. What was life like for you before you were a Christian (or during seasons when you were far from the Lord)? What hindrances kept you from taking a stand for racial unity when you were in that state of mind?

---

4. What new possibilities for racial unity are available now as a result of the gospel and the power of the Holy Spirit living in you?

THE BIG IDEA

Being reconciled to God the Father through His Son, Jesus, and walking in the power of the Holy Spirit provide the necessary foundation for authentic racial unity.

HOMEWORK (5 MINUTES)

This week, keep an eye out for invitations to participate in racial reconciliation. Answer the following questions, and come prepared to discuss your answers with the group next week.

- In what areas are you noticing an invitation to participate in the work of racial reconciliation?

____

____

____

- What steps are being put forth in the area of racial reconciliation from ministries or friends in your social media feeds?

____

____

____

- Do you see these steps as helping or hindering unity?

____

____

____

- Do you notice any fundamental presuppositions embedded within the work or steps of racial reconciliation?

____

____

____

We've created this brief video guide to assist you in remembering key concepts as you watch the videos for each section. Fill in the blanks to complete the key concepts outlined in the video.

VIDEO GUIDE*

Why are we talking about ________ _____________ instead of _________ and ______?

The foundation must be _________ and who ___________ declares we are.

We are _____________. We are ____________.

If we don't understand this first, we will never have a true reason to stand *against* secular frameworks and *for* the truth of Scripture or an understanding of why we are to do so.

Misconception: Christians can't have racial unity ______ we have racial reconciliation.

- You must do the work of racial reconciliation.
- _______ can't happen without racial reconciliation.

Reconciliation: According to culture, reconciliation is the idea of bringing different races (especially blacks and whites) together to discuss the _____ ___________ of the past and present and to begin a way forward to healing and relationship between the two groups.

It's not that racial reconciliation is unattainable; it's that racial reconciliation is the wrong goal.

2 Corinthians 5 tells us to "be _______." Paul says that we have been given the ministry of reconciliation.

Paul is not describing reconciliation between two __________ sinful groups.

Paul describes reconciliation between a ___________ ___________ and a _______ _______.

Racial unity can begin only when our __________ are in right relationship with God.

**Note the answer key provided on page 71.*

Notes

LESSON 2

WHO DO YOU THINK YOU ARE?

WARM UP

Take 10 minutes to discuss last week's homework.

To keep our sharing focused on the lesson, group members who weren't able to complete the homework should limit their participation to listening during this discussion time.

The 2020 United States census invites us to self-identify in one of five racial categories: White, Black or African American, American Indian or Alaska Native, Asian, or Pacific Islander. For many, identifying as a member of one of these groups means taking pride in their ethnicity. For others, such a grouping may cause shame. Still others find that their ethnicity isn't even listed. In culture and the media, some of these groups are highlighted and promoted, while others are ridiculed, demeaned, or ignored altogether.

In this lesson, we'll consider the question "What role does ethnicity have in the life of a Christian?"

OPENING DISCUSSION (10 MINUTES)

Most of us have multiple identities. When meeting someone new, we may ask questions such as "What do you do for a living?" or "How many children do you have?"

1. What do you consider your primary identity? Is it your occupation? Your family situation? Your gender? Your ethnicity or cultural heritage?

____

____

____

2. What major "tribes" (groups) do you belong to? Are they based on a hobby? Your political affiliation or religion? Your ethnicity or cultural heritage?

____

____

____

3. What do you enjoy about your ethnic heritage?

____

____

____

Cultural shifts can be fickle. Depending on the current cultural tide, your "tribe" may be vaulted to the top, or it may plummet to the bottom. If you're on top, you're preferred and honored and enjoy a coveted status. If you're on the bottom, you face judgment, ridicule, and suspicion—and this can lead to disdain, shame, and resentment.

What does the Bible say about our core identity?

BIBLE STUDY (35 MINUTES)

Some critical passages of Scripture describe our core identity from God's point of view, both past and present.

1. Select someone to read Genesis 1:26–27 aloud. How do these verses describe all humans—both male and female? (Note: The Bible uses this description only for humans, never for animals. Do you think this is important? Why or why not?)

2. Select someone to read Ephesians 2:1–3 and 11–12 aloud. Next, list the terms the apostle Paul used to describe us before we were Christians. How many can your group come up with?

3. Select someone to read Ephesians 2:4–10, 13, and 19–22 aloud. Next, list the terms Paul used to describe who we are now that the gospel is changing us. How many can your group come up with?

4. Break into groups of two or three, and assign each group one of the following passages: Romans 6, Romans 8, 2 Corinthians 5:16–21, and 1 Peter 2:9–10. Each group should read their assigned passage and then list at least ten words used to describe

our identity from God's point of view. Afterward, regroup and share what each small group found.

5. Notice Paul's words in 2 Corinthians 5:16–17. In Christ, we are a new creation, and we are no longer to regard one another from a human or worldly point of view. In other words, no matter what label the world puts on us, we are now to regard one another with the labels *God* puts on us. How can this mindset change the way you act or the words you use?

All humans are created in the image of God. Adam's sin separated us from the Creator, making us an object of His wrath. But the moment we enter the household of God, the Father sees us according to our new identity—that of His children. All other identities spoken over us, especially those that the world tries to place on us, take a back seat to the identity given us by our heavenly Father. We are God's children before we're American; African; Asian; male or female; rich or poor; "butcher, baker or candlestick maker"; or any other identifier. This idea goes directly against a culture seeking to categorize people by ethnicity, socioeconomic status, gender, or something else.

TEACHING (15 MINUTES)

The teaching portion of this lesson builds on our study. Here are a few key points to listen for as you watch:

- Only humans are created in the image of God. This truth is foundational to our dignity, value, and worth.
- All humans are either "in Adam" or "in Christ."
- As Christians, we are children of God. This is our primary identity.
- In Christ, there is now "neither Jew nor Greek," rich nor poor, male nor female. This is because we are all "one new man" with the true nature of our identity in Christ.
- We are not to regard fellow Christians according to the "old" man (worldly labels).

- When someone attempts to persuade you to accept a false identity, you can be confident that your identity is found in Jesus.

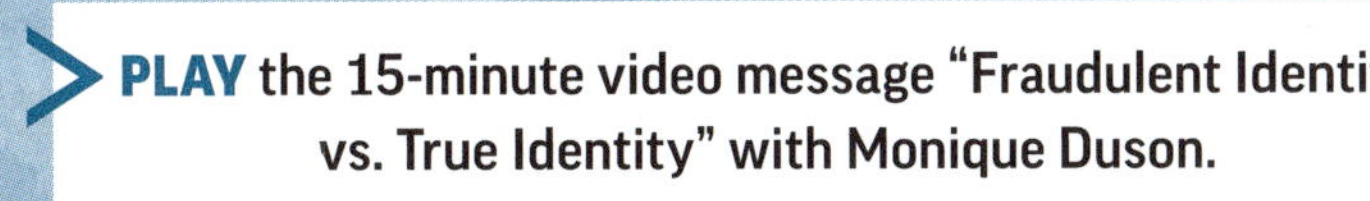

REFLECTION (15 MINUTES)

After watching the video, take a few minutes to process the teaching and hear from each other.

1. How have you seen others in your church community or within the larger evangelical community adopt unbiblical narratives about people of specific ethnic groups?

____

____

____

2. Discuss any false or fraudulent (unbiblical) identities that you've heard people speak over you or your ethnic group (e.g., racist, fragile, oppressed, victim, thug, colonized, violent). Discuss how those labels made you feel or how they affected your life. What are the harmful effects of adopting this cultural narrative?

____

____

____

3. As Christ-followers, we want our words to reflect our heavenly Father's descriptions about ourselves and others (see James 3:9–11) because we will be held accountable for every careless word (see Matthew 12:35–37). Discuss a time when you used careless words to speak an unbiblical identity over someone or a group of people. This may include telling jokes about people of a different ethnicity or even your own ethnicity.

____

____

____

4. In what ways have you adopted the cultural narrative regarding yourself or your ethnic group, or regarding someone else or their ethnic group? (Examples: "I'm just a white man." "I'll never break through the glass ceiling.") What verses in this lesson change that? Can you think of other verses that apply?

THE BIG IDEA

Christians need to seek their identity in Scripture first. We must allow ourselves to be defined by the One who formed and foreknew us.

HOMEWORK (5 MINUTES)

Throughout this week, take inventory of how many times you're labeled—by yourself or by others. This might include labels that describe members of your ethnic group.

- What are the specific labels being placed on you?

- Which labels do you agree with? Which ones do you disagree with? Why?

- What emotions do these labels evoke?

VIDEO GUIDE*

Fill in the blanks to complete the key concepts outlined in the video.

Let's talk about the ________ of who we are.

Fraudulent Identity: Identity that goes against how we are identified in ____________.

Racial reconciliation invites us to adopt a _________ ___________, to believe something about ourselves that is outside of what Scripture says about us.

In Scripture, we see that we are reconciled through the work of Christ.

According to antiracism and CRT: black people are part of an oppressed class of people and the constant victim of America's racist structures. White people are racist, fragile, oppressors, guilty of racism by way of complicity, and privileged. These are fake identities!

God had already given Eve an _____________.

In John 1:12 Scripture identifies those who believe in Christ as _________ of _________.

Our ethnic identity takes a back seat to our new identity. Our new identity is found in _______ first.

_____________ defines us as chosen, a royal priesthood, brothers and sisters, children of God, redeemed.

___________ defines us as oppressor, oppressed, privileged, victim, nonbinary, white supremacist, racist, white adjacent, ally, Christian privileged, ableist, fragile, antiracist, abolitionist, and many other such identifiers.

False identities subvert who God says we are.

_____ ________ who the Father says we are. _____ ______ His children. _____ _______ reconciled. We are family.

Note the answer key provided on page 71.

Notes

LESSON 3

WHAT DOES IT MEAN TO BE FAMILY?

WARM UP

Take 10 minutes to discuss last week's homework.

To keep our sharing focused on the lesson, group members who weren't able to complete the homework should limit their participation to listening during this discussion time.

Our world is racially divided. Even churches reflect this problem. Secular culture offers little hope of racial unity because it has no foundation for it. As Christians, our hearts should be grieved at the level of racial disunity and infighting within our churches. Why? Because we have a different model in Scripture, plus the power of the Holy Spirit, to lead us into authentic racial unity.

In this lesson, we'll consider the question "What is the foundation for racial unity in the Church?"

OPENING DISCUSSION (10 MINUTES)

There are many calls right now for Christians to engage in the work of racial reconciliation. But, as we learned in Lesson 1, the biblical support for that idea is thin. And, according to what we learned in Lesson 2, Christians have a new identity. This clarity—the understanding that all believers are God's children—ought to shape the way we think about ourselves and others.

1. Unfortunately, God's people are still very divided. Why?

____

____

____

2. What do you see as potential obstacles to unity in your local church? What barriers separate fellow believers?

____

____

____

God says we have a new identity. But we are still divided. Let's talk about it.

BIBLE STUDY (35 MINUTES)

Several critical passages of Scripture describe our relationship to one another in the Church.

1. Select someone to read Ephesians 1:3–14 aloud. Describe God's design for His people to be united. What analogy does He use in verse 5 to describe our relationship to one another?

2. Select someone to read Ephesians 2:11–22 aloud. Describe the mystery that brings unity to God's new humanity.

3. Ephesians 2 teaches that the dividing wall that once separated Jews and Gentiles (religious and ethnic enemies) was destroyed by the work of Jesus. No more work needed to be done before acknowledging that they were one new people. How would this same principle apply to our current situation in the Church today?

4. Read the following verses aloud. What cultural barriers to unity are eliminated through the work of Christ?

    - Colossians 3:1–11

- 1 Timothy 5:1–2

God has a unique design for family, both physically and spiritually. Ephesians 1:3–14 lays out His design for His family: a unified body of believers brought together through the sacrifice of Jesus Christ. All ethnic groups now have access to God the Father through Jesus, creating one new family out of many peoples and ethnicities.

TEACHING (15 MINUTES)

The teaching portion of this lesson builds on our Bible study. Here are a few key points to listen for as you watch the video:

- All humans are created in the image of God. This truth gives us our inherent value, dignity, and worth. See Genesis 1:26–27, Genesis 9:5–6, and James 3:8–9.

Who Were the Scythians?

WHY DID PAUL refer to the Scythians in Colossians 3? They were an ancient civilization of warring nomads. You can look them up. The Scythians are sort of interesting.

When Paul wrote to the Colossians about putting on their new self or claiming their new identity, he revealed that their former enemies on the battlefield had become their brothers and sisters. Those who may even have had relatives killed by these barbarians had become spiritual family members. Then, as now, our identity in Christ is foundational. This reality guides and shapes how we see ourselves and all fellow believers. Oppressed and oppressors have become brothers and sisters. We must stop thinking of ourselves in worldly ways. In Christ, we are united as one.

- Not all humans are children of God. That title is reserved exclusively for those who enter into a covenant relationship with the Father.
- Family is God's declaration of a spiritual reality. We are expected to live out this reality in the physical world.
- God decides who is included in His family. Our job is to live together as a family.
- Through Christ, we have freedom to love.

PLAY the 15-minute video message "We Are Family" with Monique Duson.

REFLECTION (15 MINUTES)

After watching the video, take a few minutes to process the teaching and hear from each other.

1. What did you find helpful about the teaching?

____

____

____

2. Share one idea from the teaching that was new for you. What other questions does that new idea raise?

____

____

____

3. If Christians were to consider each other as brothers and sisters first—before taking into account skin color, ethnicity, or cultural background—what new possibilities do you think would become available in your relationships?

____

____

____

4. What thoughts/actions are either added or removed when you see someone as a brother or sister first?

THE BIG IDEA

Through Jesus, we've been adopted into the family of God and are now brothers and sisters. This was God's plan from the beginning. When we view Christians as family first, rather than according to their skin color, ethnicity, or cultural background, we guard against suspicion and bias and cultivate a greater space for love, humility, curiosity, and empathy.

HOMEWORK (5 MINUTES)

Read the entire book of Ephesians this week. Reflect each day on the fact that, as Christians, we are brothers and sisters. Notice any shifts in your attitude, thoughts, or prayers as you consider the reality that those in your circle or church community are not just fellow church members but family.

VIDEO GUIDE*

Fill in the blanks to complete the key concepts outlined in the video.

Review: We are __________ of God. We are created to live as ________.

While all humans are created in the image of God, spiritually, not all humans are called the children of God. The identity of "_______ ___ ______" is reserved for those in the family of God.

Ephesians 1:5 (NLT): "God decided in advance to adopt us into his own family by bringing us to himself through Jesus Christ. This is what he wanted to do, and it gave him great pleasure."

The family of God is now _________ - _________!

Family is God's _______________ of a spiritual __________. We see this concept in the process of _______________.

The narrative pushed in culture today is that ________-_________ adoption is damaging to children.

Adoption is a living picture of what God has created through the work of His Son on the cross.

Family gives you something to ________ ______.

Family is worth fighting for.

We are family, and we must now work to keep the ________ given to us in accordance with our familial relationship.

Pursue relationships to keep the unity.

The Body of Christ is the _____ of God. Regardless of _______ _________.

Note the answer key provided on page 71.

Notes

LESSON 4

HOW DO WE WALK IN UNITY?

WARM UP

Take 10 minutes to discuss last week's homework.

To keep our sharing focused on the lesson, group members who weren't able to complete the homework should limit their participation to listening during the homework discussion time.

Family is the foundation for community. From the beginning, God's original design for humanity was that we'd live within family. Adam and Eve are our first parents. God told Adam and Eve to be fruitful, multiply, and subdue and rule the earth (Genesis 1:28).

As members of God's household, we are first and foremost brothers and sisters. This is an objective truth, a declared reality by our heavenly Father about *who* we are in relationship to one another.

But *"Hello, sin!"* Being a family doesn't automatically mean that all the siblings get along with each other.

In this lesson, we'll consider the question "How do members of the family walk in unity with each other?"

OPENING DISCUSSION (10 MINUTES)

The family context is one of the most vital pictures God chose to describe His vision for the Church. But our sinfulness keeps us from consistently living out His plan.

1. What do you see as potential obstacles to considering each other as family?

2. How much of this disunity is due to legitimate doctrinal differences versus divisions based on personal preferences or narratives of the majority culture?

If God describes us as family, what does that mean for our life together in the local church? What does it mean for participation with other churches in your community? Let's talk about it.

BIBLE STUDY (35 MINUTES)

Let's take a closer look at some critical passages of Scripture that describe how we're to treat one another in the Church.

1. Select someone to read John 17 (yes, the entire chapter) aloud. Describe Jesus's vision for His people. How is His vision to be achieved? What is the work of the Holy Spirit in the believers' pursuit of unity?

____

____

____

2. Select someone to read aloud Ephesians 4:1–6, 11–17, and 29–32 aloud. How are Christians instructed to "keep the unity"?

____

____

____

3. What is the basis for unity in verses 13–14?

____

____

____

4. Select someone to read Ephesians 4:20–32 aloud (the final verses in this section have already been read, but the emphasis here is different). How are Christians told to put off their "old self" and walk in the reality of being a new creation? How would practicing these behaviors contribute toward unity in the Body?

____

____

____

Unity Around the Truth

IN THE GOSPEL OF JOHN, Jesus prayed these words for His disciples: "They are not of the world, even as I am not of it. Sanctify them by the truth; your word is truth. As you sent me into the world, I have sent them into the world. For them I sanctify myself, that they too may be truly sanctified." (John 17:16-19)

Here, the word "sanctify" can also be translated as "separate." Jesus's prayer is that His followers would be separated from the world by the truth of the Word. We see that Christ-followers are not *of* the world. But what are we to be separated *to*? A couple of verses later, Jesus says:

> ". . . that all of them may be one, Father, just as you are in me and I am in you. May they also be in us so that the world may believe that you have sent me." (John 17:21)

We are being separated *to* Christ, *to* the Father, *and to* each other by the power of the Holy Spirit.

The next two verses are also significant:

> "I have given them the glory that you gave me, that they may be one as we are one—I in them and you in me—so that they may be brought to complete unity. Then the world will know that you sent me and have loved them even as you have loved me." (John 17:22-23)

The unity we must keep is found in the truth of God's Word. In 1 Corinthians 1, Paul appeals to the church at Corinth to be perfectly united in the areas in which it matters most—in mind and in thought. Walking in unity is about keeping the tenets of the faith as a first priority. Paul implored the Corinthians to unite around Scripture and the truth of Jesus Christ so that they would have no divisions among themselves. Uniting around a false belief or heretical idea would certainly lead to division.

Christians are separated *from* the world by the Word of God. And again, they are called *to* Jesus, *to* our Heavenly Father, and *to* one another. This is not an easy calling, but we have been endowed with the ability to walk in unity through the power of the Holy Spirit.

5. Select someone to read Galatians 5:13–26 aloud. In light of God's command to love our neighbor, what does love look like according to God's Word? What attitudes of the heart are described? How would those attitudes affect our actions when it comes to living in unity with one another as Christians?

___

___

___

If we are serious about racial unity, we must conform our thoughts, emotions, and actions to biblical truth. We cannot have unity—racially or otherwise—without first having a solid foundation. Shared beliefs build a platform for unity. For Christians, these beliefs must be rooted and grounded in historic Christianity.

TEACHING (15 MINUTES)

The teaching portion of this lesson builds on our Bible study. Here are a few key points to listen for as you watch the video:

- Your efforts to bring about racial reconciliation may look more like the deeds of the flesh than the fruit of the Spirit. What happens when this occurs?
- Diversity can actually bring unity.
- Love isn't vague. *Love* is spelled out in Scripture.
- Love is practical; it can't just be an abstract idea or a platitude.
- A person empowered by the Holy Spirit will not have a chronically reactive posture.

PLAY the 15-minute video message "Walking in Unity" with Monique Duson.

REFLECTION (15 MINUTES)

After watching the video, take a few minutes to process the teaching and hear from each other.

1. What barriers prevent Christians from achieving unity?

___

___

___

2. What obstacles do you put up before trusting people from other cultures or ethnicities? Be specific.

3. Discuss a time when you had a conversation about ethnic or cultural differences that didn't go well.

- In light of this study, list below two specific things you would choose to do differently today.

- Based on the Bible Study section of this chapter, list three scriptural principles that could help you love your neighbor more intentionally.

THE BIG IDEA

The Holy Spirit empowers believers to walk in unity. This unity must be built upon the truth of Scripture. We must be obedient to the truth that we are brothers and sisters. We display our obedience when we lead lives worthy of our calling, showing humility, kindness, and gentleness.

HOMEWORK (5 MINUTES)

This week's homework involves a feedback exercise. Soliciting feedback is about extending an invitation for someone to share their thoughts, feelings, perceptions, or opinions about a situation. When we invite feedback about ourselves, such an invitation may require courage. Just remember: feedback should be seen as data to consider, not necessarily as undeniable fact. Sometimes people give us data that is off base or that is more about what they are going through at the time. But their input can still highlight our blind spots. If we are willing to pay attention, we can find new opportunities for growth.

For your homework, connect with at least one other person from your small group and ask the following question: "From your perspective, what are some things I do or say that may hinder unity?" Focus on listening and asking clarifying questions, or ask for concrete examples to ensure that you understand what is being said. Do *not* offer any explanations or defensive responses. Just listen to the response and then, with prayer and conversation with the Holy Spirit, evaluate it. Do you see any truth in the feedback?

VIDEO GUIDE*

Fill in the blanks to complete the key concepts outlined in the video.

How are we to walk out this ________ unity?

Culture says: Unity requires certain ________.

Works for white people: Read books about racism, repent, lament, legislate.

Works for black people: Be aware of racist systems, understand that racism is embedded in our country's culture, protest, and stay "woke."

These works are what culture requires to get us to the table of ________ __________________.

People of color decide who is ________ to come to the table to talk about reconciliation.

A biblical approach to unity has, at its foundation, a heart transformed by the ____________ and an understanding that the ______ ___________, not our own effort, empowers us.

Ephesians 4:2: "Be completely humble and gentle; be patient; _________ ______ one another in love."

Proverbs 15:33: "Wisdom's instruction is to fear the Lord, and humility comes before honor."

Proverbs 11:2: "When pride comes, then comes disgrace, but with _________ comes ________."

John 17:22–23: "I have given them the glory that you gave me, that they may be one as we are one—I in them and you in me—so that they may be brought to _________ _______. Then the world will know that you sent me and have loved them even as you have loved me."

God's truth is that we _____ brothers and sisters.

We _____ share the same responsibilities to walk in unity—together.

We ______ must walk in humility, kindness, and gentleness—in fact, in all the fruits of the Spirit.

We _____ must extend generous forgiveness.

We are family first!

**Note the answer key provided on page 71.*

Notes

LESSON 5

WHAT CAN WE LEARN FROM THE EARLY CHURCH?

WARM UP

Take 10 minutes to discuss last week's homework.

To keep our sharing focused on the lesson, group members who weren't able to complete the homework should limit their participation to listening during the homework discussion time.

I have a habit of saying "Culture's gonna do what culture's gonna do." Translation: I don't expect non-Christians to act in Christ-centered ways. We live in a thoroughly post-Christian culture that operates from a godless standpoint (unless it's temporarily borrowing an idea, such as human equality, from the Christian worldview).

Keeping this in mind helps prevent me from being shocked by the maladies continuously put forth by "race experts" as paths to unity. These thought leaders usually want to build consensus around antiracism, Black Lives Matter, LGBTQ+, and reparations. We are told that only by adopting these social movements will we ever achieve racial harmony.

Sadly, many within the Church have been influenced by these secular ideas more than by the Bible. Much of what flies under the banner of "racial unity" is more consistent with secular ideas of sociology and social justice than with an intentional decision to seek the wisdom of Scripture. Well-meaning Christians are being conscripted as allies to build a type of unity in which the only goal is to overthrow those with "power" and uplift the voices of the "oppressed." The narrative asks, "If you aren't an ally in the movement, are you even a Christian?" Many evangelical churches, feeling pressure from culture, have stepped away from the historic Christian worldview and planted their feet in the soil of social justice. But culture's models for "unity" are in stark contrast to the models of unity seen in Scripture.

In this lesson, we'll consider the question "What does unity in the Body of Christ look like in real life?"

OPENING DISCUSSION (10 MINUTES)

Our culture's vision for racial unity often involves conversations of accusation, shame, and blame—which generally end up creating more division than unity.

1. Have you attended a diversity or inclusion training at your job? Or been required to read a book like *White Fragility* or *How to Be an Antiracist*?

2. Did your workplace become more racially unified after going through this experience? What has been the lasting impact? Share your story.

BIBLE STUDY (35 MINUTES)

Let's take a closer look at some critical passages of Scripture that describe how we are to treat one another in the Church.

1. Select someone to read Acts 2:42 and 4:32–37 aloud. How did members of the early Church tangibly display their love for each other? How did they cross socioeconomic lines? Make a list.

2. Select someone to read 2 Corinthians 8:1–4 and 16–20 aloud. What motivated people to share with brothers and sisters? How does the early Church provide a model of giving for us today?

3. Select someone to read Acts 5:1–11 aloud. What was the problem with Ananias and Sapphira's gift? Why did their actions cause them to be struck dead?

____

____

____

Sharing Resources

DURING THE TIME of the first-century Church, a large percentage of those living in the Roman Empire were slaves. Christians lived under a tyrannical, wicked government that demanded high taxes. Great disparities existed between the rich and the poor. Inequities were a normal way of life.

Being a Christian brought additional challenges. As the Church grew, Christians faced increasing persecution. But these challenges did not deter them; the gospel still went out! Jesus's followers corrected heresy with boldness, and the Church functioned with a clear mission. Community formed even in the midst of cultural chaos. Christians came together, holding all things in common. They shared from their combined resources. They were family. They took care of each other—not because they *had* to but because that is what had been modeled for them—first by Christ, then by the apostles. The model of the family brought them together. Jews, Gentiles, slaves, soldiers, rich, poor—such distinctions became secondary social terms. The death of Jesus unified them.

The early Church had clarity about their identity in Christ, and that clarity unified them, even through persecution and death.

Today some people point to passages of early Christians sharing resources with one another as a biblical warrant for forced sharing or socialism. But such an interpretation neglects a key component of the biblical mandate. God wants us to share with one another as an extension of our personal righteousness and our gratitude for what He has done for us, not out of compulsion or based on a government program; this kind of sharing is the result of our freewill obedience to God, motivated by love for our neighbors.

Unity in the Body of Christ cannot simply be a theoretical ideal. It must reflect the outflow of our relationship with Jesus, whose love compels us to love others with dignity. It must be a living, breathing testimony to the world that *unity is real.*

TEACHING (15 MINUTES)

The teaching portion of this lesson builds on our Bible study. Here are a few key points to listen for as you watch the video:

- Obstacles to racial unity include suspicion toward people of other ethnicities and cultures, denial of current instances of racism, and lack of meaningful relationships with people from other ethnicities and cultures.
- The foundation for biblical unity rests on sound doctrine.
- It's necessary to ask the Lord what you can do to stand for racial unity in your sphere of influence. If we are serious about racial unity, we must also be serious about our own personal righteousness and how we treat others in our daily sphere of influence.

PLAY the 15-minute video message "Our Role Model" with Monique Duson.

REFLECTION (15 MINUTES)

After watching the video, take a few minutes to process the teaching and hear from each other.

1. Discuss a time when you personally witnessed an injustice based on race. What did you do? What, if anything, would you do differently now?

___

___

___

2. Have you experienced hardship or discrimination as a direct result of your ethnicity? If so, please share your story with the group.

___

___

___

- Share three specific ways in which your local church or church friends could have supported you in that season.

- If your group includes a member of the law enforcement community (such as a police officer, border patrol agent, or prison guard), ask whether they would be willing to share three specific ways in which they try to be salt and light in a difficult profession. How do they advocate for equal treatment for all? How do they act in kindness toward those who are unkind to them?

THE BIG IDEA

There's much to be gleaned from the example of the early Church. Unity was practical and action-oriented, not simply something to be talked about, not merely a theory. Identities according to the flesh remained secondary to identity in Christ. In Christ, believers were family.

HOMEWORK (5 MINUTES)

This week's homework involves a similar feedback exercise to last week's. This time, connect with someone you know from outside your small group who has a different ethnic or cultural background, and ask the same question: "From your perspective, what are some things I do or say that may hinder racial unity?" Focus on listening. Ask clarifying questions or request concrete examples to ensure that you understand what's being said. Don't offer any explanations or defensive responses; just listen for the data. Then, with prayer and conversation with the Holy Spirit, evaluate it. Do you see any truth in the feedback?

VIDEO GUIDE*

Fill in the blanks to complete the key concepts outlined in the video.

Review: God has made us ________.

The _____ and the _____ fall far too short of the outline modeled in Scripture.

Cultural models for unity include advocacy for antiracism, Black Lives Matter, LGBTQ+, and reparations (economic justice).

Allyship: An ally is someone who makes the commitment and effort to ___________ their ________ and commits to reducing their participation in ____________.

While cultural unity is built on consensus, biblical unity is built upon the ______ of ___________.

Family doesn't let family go hungry.

Christians who are serious about racial unity also need to be serious about understanding the ________ ___ _______ and walking in their ________ ___________.

Obedience to truth requires us to be _______ and ______________.

Psalm 51:6: "Yet you desired faithfulness even in the womb; you taught me wisdom in that secret place."

Matthew 23 is Jesus's warning against _________.

Note the answer key provided on page 71.

Notes

LESSON 6

WHOSE RESPONSIBILITY IS RACIAL UNITY?

WARM UP

Take 10 minutes to discuss last week's homework.

To keep our sharing focused on the lesson, group members who weren't able to complete the homework should limit their participation to listening during the homework discussion time.

In our last week together, we are going to dive a little deeper into the practical application of all we've learned. We've already laid a solid biblical foundation for racial unity. Now, more specifically, we'll work to understand how we participate with one another. While we might think that we're standing for unity, we might, in reality, be acting in subtle ways that actually separate us from those who are different from us. As we have conversations that can result in greater racial unity, we must do so with an awareness of our own fears, emotions, and doubts. And we must ask the Lord to help us overcome them.

In this lesson, we'll consider the question "What will be my stand for racial unity?" This may be our most important conversation yet!

OPENING DISCUSSION (10 MINUTES)

Race conversations may put us on guard. We might become suspicious, defensive, and afraid. Guarding our hearts includes having wisdom to know when it is okay to trust someone or enter into friendship with them. But when we've been hurt, ridiculed, or told that our voice doesn't matter because of our ethnic heritage or the color of our skin, guarding our hearts may feel warranted. And while we may want to keep our guard up, this self-protective act can prevent racial unity from becoming part of our personal lives.

The road to greater racial unity begins with asking the Holy Spirit to reveal how we may be contributing to division.

1. How might you be acting as an obstacle to racial unity? Consider these questions:
    - Is there someone I need to forgive in this regard?
    - Do I need to ask anyone for forgiveness? If so, who?
    - What (unspoken) resentments and biases do I have against certain people or groups?
    - When I come into contact with someone from a different ethnic group, what do I think they believe about me, based on my ethnicity?

- What fears do I have about participating in conversations about race, justice, or unity with people from other ethnic groups?
- In what areas am I resistant to hearing about the difficulties of others who have experienced race-based mistreatment?

2. What can you do to overcome these obstacles?

___

___

___

BIBLE STUDY (35 MINUTES)

Let's take a closer look at some critical passages of Scripture that describe how Christians should regard each other.

1. Select someone to read the book of Philemon aloud. (Yes, the entire book.) What relationship did Philemon and Onesimus have with one another?

___

___

___

2. In verses 16–17, how did Paul instruct Philemon to regard Onesimus upon his return?

___

___

___

3. The story of Philemon is a microcosm of how Christians are to relate to one another, even when they are from different cultural or socioeconomic backgrounds. How could this model apply to our current cultural conflict about racial differences?

___

___

___

TEACHING (15 MINUTES)

The teaching portion of this lesson builds on our Bible study. Here are a few key points to listen for as you watch the video:

- People on both sides of the race conversation have fears and concerns, but we cannot allow those fears and concerns to dictate or overrule Scripture or prevent our participation with others within the Body of Christ.
- We all have the responsibility "to live a life worthy of the calling you have received" (Ephesians 4:1). This means that everyone needs to be humble, gentle, and patient, bearing with one another in love.

PLAY the 15-minute video message "Racial Unity Begins with Me" with Monique Duson.

REFLECTION (15 MINUTES)

After watching the video, take a few minutes to process the teaching and hear from each other.

To some degree, most humans have a self-preservation mechanism. When we've been hurt by someone, we can become suspicious about nearly everything else that person does. Our mistrust becomes a means for making sure we don't get hurt twice.

But suspicion can also breed contempt. Left unresolved, our protection plan can quickly become an attitude of disdain or even hatred. Soon we start saying things such as "They *always* do that" or "Those people are *all* like that." We must not overgeneralize and declare that "*all those people* are [fill in the blank]." Some people of each ethnicity are hardworking, while others are lazy. Some are kind, while others are mean. Some are wise, others misinformed or foolish. Regardless of our ethnicity, Paul instructs us to "make every effort to keep the unity" (Ephesians 4:3a) through humility, gentleness, patience, kindness, and love.

1. What suspicions or biases might you be holding against a person of another ethnicity? Would you be as suspicious if that person were of your own ethnicity?

____

____

____

Three Reasons Christians Shouldn't Participate in Racial Reconciliation Work

ONCE WE'RE ADOPTED into the family of God, there is nothing more any of us must do to become "family" with other believers. We *are* family. This declaration about our identity was made by God. It's objectively true. We've already been to court and have heard the judge proclaim that we've been adopted into God's "forever family."

This is why we have deep concerns about many of the current calls for Christians to engage in the "work" of racial reconciliation.

1. Christians have already been brought together through adoption. When we were adopted into the family of God, He reconciled us to Himself and brought us together as brothers and sisters. As God's children, we are already reconciled to each other.

2. Ethnic division is everyone's problem. Many conversations about racial reconciliation focus on telling white people about their responsibilities. The onus for reconciling usually rests on the shoulders of white brothers and sisters. In part, this may be due to a fundamental assumption, held by many social justice advocates, that Black, Indigenous, and People of Color (BIPOC) are already doing the work. Now it's time, they say, for white people to "come to the table." But from God's viewpoint, the work has already been done. Everyone has a mutual responsibility to walk in humility, forgive others, and treat one another as brothers and sisters. No one individual has a greater burden than another to do the work simply because of the melanin content of their skin.

3. The work of racial reconciliation removes God from the equation. The term "reconciliation" has been redefined in many evangelical spaces. "Reconciliation to God" has been shifted to "reconciliation among people groups." Often the idea of reconciling to each other overlooks our foundational need to reconcile to God first. Only then can we trust that He has already reconciled us to others.

2. What can you do to begin fostering conversations about racial unity? Ideas may include visiting other church communities or hosting events that bring believers from different communities and ethnic backgrounds together. What else can you think of?

____

____

____

THE BIG IDEA

When engaging in racial unity, we must ask the Holy Spirit to reveal the attitudes in our hearts that may prevent true unity.

PSALM 139:23-24
Search me, God, and know my heart;
test me and know my anxious thoughts.
See if there is any offensive way in me,
and lead me in the way everlasting.

We aren't always aware of those attitudes, but the Lord certainly is. We must repent of our attitudes, actions, and inactions that prevent unity. Racism or race-based favoritism is a sin, but it's not an unpardonable sin. Once we see what He sees in us, we will be able to treat others, regardless of their ethnicity, as brothers and sisters.

VIDEO GUIDE*

Fill in the blanks to complete the key concepts outlined in the video.

Critical Race Theory

- This model for unity has many of its foundational tenets in ________ and ____-__________ ideology.
- CRT organizes people into varying groups based on different social criteria, such as male or female, white or person of color, racist or antiracist, and privileged or oppressed.
- Understanding your __________ or working for the ____________ result of all people is how unity is derived.

According to this theory, equity can be attained by:

- Acknowledging your ____________ in racism or participation in _____________.
- Forced redistribution of __________ or ___________.

According to CRT, ________, not __________, is the goal.

Biblical Unity Model

- Unity begins when we come into ___________ with Jesus.
- Our hearts are ______________ by Him and the _________ of the Holy Spirit.
- We are all called to obey Jesus's commands to ______ our neighbor.
- We find out _________ to love our neighbor by looking at God's eternal moral law.

God's model for unity also calls His people to be aware of what's happening in their __________ and to treat others _______.

Practical Breakdown of the Biblical Unity Model

#1 - Come into relationship with ________.

#2 - Have a _______ transformed by Jesus and the Holy Spirit.

#3 - Practice __________ ______________ in your everyday life.

#4 - Understand what's happening in your ______________.

#5 - Get into ___________ ____________ with people of other ethnicities.

Acts 10:34–35: "Then Peter began to speak: 'I now realize how true it is that God does not show __________, but accepts from every nation the one who fears him and does what is right.'"

We are family.

Note the answer key provided on page 71.

Notes

APPENDIX

DEVELOPING A BIBLICAL MODEL FOR RACIAL UNITY

Many Christian leaders and ministries are deeply committed to the work of racial reconciliation. The heart behind their efforts is a desire to ensure that everyone has an opportunity to hear the gospel and participate in the local church as equals. And that's a great thing!

But in our zeal to "do good," we must make sure that we're being biblical. A well-defined model for unity will help us build upon the biblical foundation and walk out the practical next steps. We don't want to inadvertently baptize worldly ideas with some Bible verses taken out of context in the name of racial unity and justice.

Any model for racial unity should address the following questions:

1. What is racism?

- **CULTURE SAYS** the common definition for "racism" is "prejudice plus power." According to many Critical Race Theory experts, racism is considered the ordinary, everyday experience of most people of color. According to Ibram X. Kendi, racism is the combination of "racist policies and racist ideas that produces and normalizes racial inequities" (Kendi, *How to Be An Antiracist*, p. 17).
- **HISTORIC CHRISTIANITY SAYS** that "racism" is not a biblical term. However, it could be described as some combination of (1) ethnic favoritism (either *advancing* or *disadvantaging* a person or group based on their skin color, physical features, regional accent, or cultural heritage) and (2) hatred in our hearts toward a person or group of people based on their physical features, regional accent, or cultural heritage.

2. What is the fundamental problem behind racial division?

- **CULTURE SAYS** that racism is ordinary and pervasive. Its root is America's history, with large-scale systems that have oppressed people of color and continue to marginalize and oppress them today.
- **HISTORIC CHRISTIANITY SAYS** the root of racial division is that all humans have sinful and corrupt desires. We either engage in individual acts of race-based bias, or groups of sinners collaborate to exploit others using race-based bias.

3. Is racism America's foundational problem?

- **CULTURE SAYS** that racism is America's original sin. Because white Europeans created all of the systems in our country, they were set up from the beginning to benefit Caucasians and marginalize any ethnic group without white skin. For this reason, racism pervades all systems and structures. The question is not *whether* racism is happening, but *how* it is happening. Racism is always in play. According to this thinking, racism will be removed only when systems of whiteness that perpetuate racism are eliminated.
- **HISTORIC CHRISTIANITY SAYS** that all sin is evil in God's eyes. Different sins have different consequences. The sin of racism can be forgiven as a result of Jesus's death. It is not a special sin in need of a special path of forgiveness to absolve guilt.

4. Who can be a racist?

- **CULTURE SAYS** that because institutional power belongs to white people, only white people can be racist. People of color cannot, by definition, be classified as racist.
- **HISTORIC CHRISTIANITY SAYS** that all people can perpetuate sinful acts against one another. There aren't any sins that only affect certain groups of people based on the melanin content of their skin.

5. Who can be a victim of racism?

- **CULTURE SAYS** that because people of color lack institutional power, they alone can be victims of true racism. Within the last few years, however, with the emergence of voices like Ibram X. Kendi's, the view that people of color lack power, and therefore can't be racist, is shifting. In *How to be an Antiracist,* Kendi writes, "The truth is: Black people can be racist because Black people do have power, even if limited" (p. 141).
- **HISTORIC CHRISTIANITY SAYS** that all people, regardless of ethnic or cultural background, can be victims of race-based mistreatment of others.

6. **What is the foundation for racial unity?**

- **CULTURE SAYS** that all people must commit to doing the work of antiracism, actively fighting against policies that are deemed racist due to their inequitable results. There are, however, specific tasks listed for white people. These include lamenting with people of color for past and present acts of racism committed in the United States and repenting of their whiteness—the normative, usually unseen and/or unknown set of privileges granted only to white people. Other tasks include decolonizing the Bible and Christianity, redressing history books to reflect America's history with racism from before the founding of the nation, and engaging in wealth redistribution and reparations.
- **HISTORIC CHRISTIANITY SAYS** that, as the gospel goes out to the ends of the earth, people from every nation, tribe, and tongue will come to faith in Jesus's death and resurrection and form one new people, thus becoming spiritual brothers and sisters.

7. **How do I walk in racial unity with others?**

- **CULTURE SAYS** that racial unity can be achieved only when white people understand their position and privilege within society. They must work to amplify the voices of people of color and/or of any other group considered marginalized or oppressed according to cultural normative standards.
- **HISTORIC CHRISTIANITY SAYS** that unity can be maintained only when Christians cultivate the fruit of the Spirit and resist the deeds of the flesh (Galatians 5), walk in humility (Ephesians 4:2–3), share with those in need (2 Corinthians 9:7), and engage in empathy (1 Corinthians 12:26). When an individual has committed a personal offense against a fellow Christian or has been the victim of an affront, they should go to that person in private and engage in genuine repentance and/or generous forgiveness (Matthew 18).

8. How do I build meaningful relationships with people from other ethnicities and cultures?

- **CULTURE SAYS** that meaningful relationships will result when the oppressors become allies with those in oppressed categories. This requires that white people stand up and speak out on behalf of the racially marginalized and oppressed.

- **HISTORIC CHRISTIANITY SAYS** to view other Christians in light of our new identity as brothers and sisters—and then walk in humility, gentleness, and patience, bearing with one another in love and maintaining the bond of peace (Ephesians 4).

  With non-Christians, we should be prayerful and quick to listen. We should express patience and empathy, speaking biblical truths with kindness.

9. Is racism a thing of the past?

- **CULTURE SAYS** that racism is pervasive and always present and will be eliminated only when doing so benefits those in power (white people).

- In *Critical Race Theory: An Introduction (Third Edition)*, Richard Delgado and Jean Stefancic define racism as "ordinary, not aberrational—'normal science,' the usual way society does business, the common, everyday experience of most people of color in this country" (p. 8). Further, because of what is defined as "interest convergence," there is no desire on the part of white people to eliminate racism. Advancement and eradication of antiblack racism will take place only as it benefits white people. Delgado and Stefancic write, "Because racism advances the interests of both white elites (materially) and working-class whites (psychically), large segments of society have little incentive to eradicate it" (p. 8).

- **HISTORIC CHRISTIANITY SAYS** that, as long as there are humans, there will be sin. Racism (race-based partiality) is sin. There was ethnic partiality in the opening pages of the Bible, and there will be ethnic partiality until Jesus returns and we move into the New Creation.

10. How do I stand against racial injustice?

- **CULTURE SAYS** that we must become antiracist and promote equity. People must actively work toward pressuring those in power to legislate against practices and policies that result in racial disparity or inequity and cancel anyone who is not antiracist.
- **HISTORIC CHRISTIANITY SAYS** that Christians should walk according to God's justice standards. We are not to treat people with partiality due to their ethnic heritage or culture, and we are to raise children to understand that all people have equal dignity, value, and worth. We must care for the vulnerable in our families and provide for them through hard work. Resources are to be shared with those in our local churches who are in need.
- We also need to be aware of what's happening within our communities. If we know of racist behavior from people within our churches, we should have a conversation with them and bring that information to church leadership. If we're aware of racist businesses within our community, we shouldn't support them. If a congregant has a known history of racism, the pastor must bring that person under church discipline and potentially treat them as an unbeliever.
- Racism is real. We need to use our voices, our votes, and our dollars to promote equal weights and measures through the fair and impartial treatment of others.

11. What is the end goal? Will racism ever end?

- **CULTURE SAYS** that the ultimate goal is a society in which all people are treated equitably and all people are recognized as equals, with equal rights and laws. Only when this goal becomes reality will we know that we're in a post-racial society.
- **HISTORIC CHRISTIANITY SAYS** that racism will not end until Jesus returns to judge all the nations and we move into the New Creation. Until then, believers have the end goal of sharing the love of Jesus through our actions as we treat all people with dignity, acknowledging their intrinsic value and worth. As Christians model family, we can change the culture.

VIDEO OUTLINE ANSWER KEY

LESSON 1

being reconciled, justice, CRT
Scripture, Scripture
reconciled, family
until
Unity
reconciled
racial injustices
human
sinful heart, Holy God
hearts

LESSON 2

truth
Scripture
false identity
identity
children, God
Christ
Scripture
Culture
We are, We are, We are

LESSON 3

children, family
"children of God"
multi-ethnic
declaration, reality, adoption
inter-ethnic
fight for
unity
family, skin color

LESSON 4

family
works
racial reconciliation
worthy
gospel, Holy Spirit
humble, gentle
humility, wisdom
complete, unity
are
all
all
all

LESSON 5

family
culture, church
recognize, privilege, whiteness
truth, Scripture
words of Christ, personal righteousness
bold, courageous
hypocrisy

LESSON 6

Marxist, neo-Marxist
station, equitable
complicity, whiteness
wealth, property
equity, unity
relationship
transformed, power
love
how
community, equally
Jesus
heart
personal righteousness
community
meaningful relationships
favoritism

GLOSSARY

BY DR. JOE "J. R." MILLER

These definitions are intended for basic, lay-level use. While we strive to maintain academic integrity, not all scholars agree on key definitions. Because of this, these definitions may shift based on the scholar or source you consult.

Anti-racism: There is no neutral ground; people are either racist or anti-racist. The anti-racist must speak the right words and take action to reinvent institutions, rethink religion, and remake systems that are built on white supremacy.

Equity: The provision of resources—proportional to the need—that are required to guarantee an equal economic, social, and educational outcome to every disadvantaged group.

Ethnicity: The way a particular society perceives entire groups of people based on a shared geographic, national, religious, linguistic, or cultural identity. The social construct of ethnicity can be used by the dominant culture to maintain hierarchies of status, preference, and value.

Race: The way societies group people based on ancestry and a selection of biological traits such as skin color. The social construct of race is always used by the dominant racial group to maintain hierarchies of status, preference, and value.

Racism: The intentional or unintentional use of laws, religion, social convention, moral standards, and personal privilege to keep power in the hands of whites and to disadvantage people of color.

Social Justice: A socio-political theory that the West is marked by the imbalance of power between different groups of people based on the intersection of racial, ethnic, sexual, religious, and gender identities. Social justice seeks equal outcomes (fairness) between privileged and underprivileged groups which sometimes requires the suspension of individual needs, liberties, or rights.

Systemic Racism: The presence of Eurocentric ideals in every system of Western civilization (political, religious, legal, medical, and economic) where white self-interest is used as the normative ideal to disempower non-white races.

Tolerance: Is commonly defined as a willingness to accept people for their differences. However, tolerance is often a tactic of moral persuasion used in the self-interest of whites to excuse racism, make the oppressed feel guilty, and persuade people of color to remain 'tolerant' of injustice.

White Fragility: A range of defensive emotional responses—from confusion or outrage to complete denial—expressed by white people when confronted with issues of injustice or by their own complicity with systemic racism.

White Privilege: The unfair, and often covert, advantages white people have which pervades every social system, institution (public and private), and relationship. White privilege is part of the power system that protects white people from all forms of racial or ethnic discrimination.

Woke: An awareness of the ongoing need to remain vigilant for any signs of racism or other social inequity against LGBTQ+, immigrants, women, or marginalized peoples.

RECOMMEND RESOURCES

If you would like to do a deeper dive on issues related to race and justice, here are some recommendations.

Center for Biblical Unity promotes a biblical model of racial unity within the church, centering around the model of one race, one people, one Savior.

- Podcast: "All the Things"
- Podcast: "Off Code"
- Blog: https://www.centerforbiblicalunity.com

Dr. Thaddeus Williams is a theologian, university professor, and advocate for biblical justice.

- Book: *Confronting Injustice without Compromising Truth: 12 Questions Christians Should Ask about Social Justice*
- Blog: www.thaddeuswilliams.com/

Dr. Harold Felder is an apologist who addresses arguments used to support the idea that Christianity and the Bible are incompatible with people of color.

- Book: *The African American Guide to the Bible*
- Ministry: Giving an Answer https://givingananswer.org/

Dr. Neil Shenvi is a theoretical chemist and Christian apologist who focuses on critical theory, atheism, and science.

- Blog, videos, and book reviews: https://shenviapologetics.com/

Dr. Joe Miller is a Ratio Christi campus minister and co-founder of Center for Cultural Apologetics (CFCA)

- Ministry: Center for Cultural Apologetics (CFCA) https://centerforculturalapologetics.org/about/